Wilted Flowers
By Divi Maggo

Divi Maggo

Wilted Flowers

Divi Maggo

Wilted Flowers

For all the wallflowers, the *sensitive* kids
that put others' needs before theirs.

For all the misused, abused and hurt kids
that cried themselves to sleep every night.

For all the kids that grew up
but still broken from inside.

This one's for you.

Divi Maggo

Contents

Divi Maggo

Feel

"Isn't it strange that we talk *least* about the things we think about the *most*?"

Don't hate me but I will make you cry.
I want to see the hurt flowing through the tears,
the feelings you never shared with anybody.
Adding a Spotify playlist
to make you feel everything that you have run
away from most of your life.

Divi Maggo

Wilted Flowers

Grab a glass of wine or some hot tea,
a box of tissues and get ready to feel every inch of the
hurt you have been trying to lock away in a box since
you were a kid.

Let's sit down and let yourself feel.
No questions of "why", "how" or "why me".
Just sit in your feeling.

The hurt needs your time and attention,
You have tried locking it away,
Did it work?

Now let it flow - through your veins
Write it down, free your pain
And release them through your tears.

*I have added journal prompts throughout the book to
help you direct your pain, feel it fully and for once,
do yourself a favor - do not dissociate.*

Divi Maggo

Wilted Flowers

I love my mother,
but I don't like her.

I wish I did,
I wish we were best friends.

But we are not.
her words cut like knife,
I drown in her expectations.

I was never a perfect daughter,
but I tried to be.

I tried and tried until I couldn't be.
I had to choose myself.
I had to get out.

She says she loves me,
but she despises me.

Divi Maggo

For all the people that grew up listening,
I will give you something to cry about!

Do you cry at everything now?
Sad, angry, overwhelmed,
always trying to make a point?

When we needed a hug,
we were screamed at,
humiliated and belittled.

Were we that tough to love?

What was the one childhood experience that still hurts you the most? The one that goes on and on in your head in a loop almost everyday.

_____

_____

_____

_____

_____

_____

_____

_____

_____

_____

_____

_____

Divi Maggo

You can leave a broken home,
but a broken home never leaves you.

You can leave your toxic mom,
but you will still search for her love,
and feel guilty when you find it.

You can leave your angry father,
but you will carry his anger in your heart forever.

You can leave a broken home,
but a broken home never leaves you.

How to spot an adult with childhood trauma?

Leg shaking,
one earphone always off
to keep track of the *feel* of the house.

Knowing you are about to be yelled at by the way
someone's footsteps *feel* while walking.

Numb to yelling,
but crying secretly when alone.

Crying when someone finally asks,
are you okay?

Hugs make you feel uncomfortable.

Divi Maggo

The world is tough,
so you became my first bully.

The world is tough,
so you never wiped my tears.

The world is tough,
so you gave me things to cry about.

The world is tough,
so you made me hate coming home.

The world was supposed to be tough.

But you were supposed to be my shelter,
my home full of warmth and love.

Wilted Flowers

My mother's love language is criticism.

I tell her what I love,
she tells me how much she hates.

Never a positive thought,
never appreciation,
never words of love or kindness.

All she sees in everything is negativity and lack.

It is exhausting.

Divi Maggo

My mother sacrificed her dreams,
so that I could dream.

But I wish she had not.

It made her bitter and angry.
shouting and screaming from dawn to dusk.

She was drowning in society's expectations of her.
I was drowning trying to make her happy.

Little by little we both lost love for each other.

I miss her.

If you had to describe your childhood in one word, what would it be and why?
What word <u>should</u> have described your childhood instead?

Divi Maggo

The first time I was sexually assaulted,
I was nine years old.

I wish I could tell you
that was the first and the last time,
but it was not.

I could not even comprehend what had happened,
why it happened.

I told my mother,
she shoved it under the rug,
like all her problems.

I do not blame her.
she did not know what to do.

I remember my mother asking her sisters what to do.

All she heard,

Kids forget! Don't worry about it.

What will people think?

Do you want your kid to be called a victim all her life?

But I did not forget.

I wish I did.
But I did not.

Replayed in my head over and over,
all day everyday.

It still replays in my head almost everyday,
twenty years later.

I don't cry about it now,
rage has replaced tears.

Vengeance runs in my veins.

I want to shout from the rooftops.

No one can silence me now,
not even my own mother.

Divi Maggo

The little girl that tried to be perfect,
but never was.

The little girl that cried herself to sleep every night,
thinking now she needs to make her mother happy
tomorrow.

Crushing in the burden,
the tears burning in her eyes.

The little girl asking god to end it all,
would be better to have no daughter
than an imperfect one.

I am sorry I was unkind to you,
I am sorry I never spoke up.

I am sorry I never wiped your tears.

I am sorry I never let you be happy
without the burden of her expectations.

I am sorry no one noticed us drowning everyday.

I am sorry no one saved us.

I am sorry.

Wilted Flowers

I haven't slept properly since I was nine years old.

Since your brother did what he did to me.
It hurt to pee, I was just a little girl.

I told you everything,
and I waited and waited every night,
that you will come and hug me.

But you never did.
I cried myself to sleep,
hoping you will see how life drained out of my eyes.

But you never did.

*If you or anyone you know has been a victim of sexual
assault, call 800.656.HOPE (4673).*

Divi Maggo

I feel my mother would have been happy
if she had gotten off the hamster wheel.

The hamster wheel of dead end job,
not going after your dreams.

I feel she would have been softer
and warm with kind words.

I dread I will never be able to get off the hamster wheel
myself.

That I will turn like her.

And that would be the biggest regret of my life.

Wilted Flowers

My father was my first heartbreak,
my mother was my first bully.

The house never felt like home,
walking on eggshells day in and day out.

We were a perfect family from outside,
but inside everyone was living a slow death.

Divi Maggo

What do you do when your sibling is a narcissist?

The one that you shared all your giggles growing up.

Endless snow fights, hot cocoa, beach trips,
pillow fights, late night conversations.

What do you do when they end up like your narcissist
parent?

Little by little the giggles get blurry,
replaced by tears, boundaries and heartbreak.

Has the toxicity in your family affected the relationship with your siblings? Has it gotten better or worse since you started healing?

Divi Maggo

You will be called *weak* for setting boundaries.

Selfish prick!

What did we do to deserve this?

I never said that, it's all in your head.

They will gaslight you,
they will put you in a corner,
they will make you feel
there is something wrong with you.

But when the fog clears and your head is above water,
you will be glad you chose yourself.

Wilted Flowers

The youngest child wound.

The never taken seriously child.

Always have to respect your elder siblings,
even when they are wrong.

Even when they are disrespectful.

Getting the least attention and respect
but stuck with the family's toxicity the longest.

Always getting compared to the other siblings.

Whatever you do is never enough.

Divi Maggo

My mother said she did her best to raise me,
but did she?

I was called a *fat cow* almost everyday.

Why did God punish me with an ugly daughter?
My mom used to wail.

Screaming from dawn to dusk,
I used to cry myself to sleep.

My father says *your mother loved you very much.*

Was that love?

When did her love change to anger and disgust?

Wilted Flowers

You are expecting too much
from your narcissistic mother.

Did you think she will get better for your kids?

Did you think she will still love your kids
when she can not control them or flaunt them around?

Did you hope she would not judge you and your kids
when they say no or have a meltdown?

Little girl, you need to stop hoping and praying.

Divi Maggo

I might be the one going no contact.

But at the end of the day,
I just want my mom to hug me and tell me she loves me.

And I just want to cry in her arms
for all the times I cried alone growing up.

Once, just once, I want her to say
she is proud of me,
and she understands me.

She says she talks to God all the time,
but does she ever talk to him about me?

Does she ever pray for our relationship to get better?

Wilted Flowers

We gave you house, clothes, food
What else did you need?

You were never spanked or hit,
Why are you still complaining?

Is that how you measure parenting?
That you gave us basic needs
to survive and did not physically abuse us?

We needed love, affection,
kind words and softer glances.

We needed to feel safe and not walk on eggshells.

Your words cut like knives.
You called me weak everytime I cried.
The sparkle in my eyes was gone
and you did not care.

All you cared about was obedience and control.

Divi Maggo

Mother's day is difficult for me.

It always makes me think
about my mother as a woman going through life.

Not my mother yet but a person with hopes and dreams.

When did it all change?
How did it all change?

I don't think she wanted to be a bad mother.

I don't think she *knows* she is one.

It was mostly rosy until I was nine years old
and then it all changed in a moment.

Was it because I was sexually assaulted by your brother?
And you could not protect me?

I know you blamed me and you blamed yourself.

The assault did not hurt as much,
But what did hurt was how you reacted afterwards.

You became distant and angry.
Screaming all day long.

The angrier you became,
the quieter I became.

Wilted Flowers

There were weeks
where I did not say more than two words to you.

And you did not care.

I was a happy girl before
who used to talk and sing and dance.

And you did not notice when I stopped all that?

You asked me to not tell dad,
you asked me to not tell anyone.
You made me feel shameful.

All you cared about were my grades.
Your *golden child.*
Your *life's work.*
So I became obsessed with my grades.

Maybe that will make mom happy.
Maybe I will get my mom back.

But nothing was ever enough for you,
Nothing made you happy.

You made me lose friends,
I had no one to talk to at school or at home.
Honestly I don't know how I am still alive.

Divi Maggo

I know you are not a bad person,
but you were a bad mother.

Not that I have kids,
I realized how wrong all of that was.
I could never look at my kids
and say those horrible words you said to me.

But it's Mother's Day.
So I want to thank you.

Thank you for making me a better mom for my kids.

Thank you for showing me what *not* to do as a mother.

I am healing and will continue to heal for my kids.

The little girl in me still hopes
we have a better relationship.

And she will keep hoping until her last breath.

Wilted Flowers

Why is Mother's Day so hard?

Why does it bother me so much?
Looking at all the happy pictures.

Where is my *happy* mother?
I wish her a Mother's Day and we both know it's hollow.

As hollow and lifeless as our relationship.
When I was little I used to wish that our relationship
would be better when I grew up.

It will always be a dream it seems.

Divi Maggo

Mom,
in another life,
we would have been best friends.

Two girls laughing through life,
and no one feels worthless.

Maybe we will try again in the next lifetime.

How do you feel on Mother's/ Father's day?
Don't hold back - I know the feelings are heavy
and complex.

Divi Maggo

Did you also have an eggshell mother?

Did the whole house mood depend on her mood?

Were you hyper vigilant
of her slight change in emotions?

Did you miss your entire childhood
trying to make her happy?

But nothing you did was enough.
Nothing made her happy.

Did you also have an eggshell mother?
I am so sorry if you did.

Wilted Flowers

I will never be a kiss ass to my children.

Meaning I don't like to see my kids as grown adults,
with their own opinions and decisions.

I will view them standing up for themselves
and creating boundaries as disrespectful.

And find ways to play the victim.
I will isolate them
and punish them for *being disrespectful.*

My kids abandoned me in my old age.

Oh! I thought you wanted us to stay away from you.

I am sorry
if you also have emotionally immature parents.

Divi Maggo

Your heart breaks every time you have a
I need my mom moment.

Because she was your first heartbreak,
your first bully.

The first person who stifled your voice,
called you *weak* for having emotions.

Who do you go to when you have
I need my mom moments?

When your mom is still alive but she is dead inside?

Who do you go to when you have "I need my mom" moments?

Divi Maggo

It's a constant tug of war
between my inner child and the inner teenager.

The inner child still wants to keep the peace,
wants validation that she will never get.

And the inner teenager wants to burn this
whole toxic family dynamic to the ground.

Wilted Flowers

My family's generational curse is unkindness.

Unkind words, harsh voices.
screaming, shouting, arguing.

They wear it like a badge of honor.

And they expect everyone to *forget*.
Sweep it under the rug and never talk about it.

No matter how much it hurts.
And they never change
no matter how many boundaries you create.

Divi Maggo

I don't find peace with my blood family.

And this is the most heartbreaking part of my life.

It's sad that the people who birthed me
are the reason for most of my tears.

All my life I chose them,
their peace and happiness.

Hoping they will see the pain in my eyes
and ask me if I am okay.

But they never did.

Wilted Flowers

You mom did not want a kid,
she wanted a trophy.

Someone that will achieve *her* dream life.
At last, a *thing* she can be proud of.

Cure her physical, emotional and financial insecurities.

Make her feel superior.

But her kids are also broken just like her.
All her unhealed trauma staring back at her.

And souls craving a mother's love.

Divi Maggo

My mother only acknowledged me
when I did something to make her proud.

I could feel her eyes judging me across the room,
the pressure of being perfect.

It still aches my soul
that I had to *perform* to feel loved.

The shame I used to feel for not being good enough.

The little girl used to worship you,
it's heartbreaking how much you hurt her.

She has neither beauty nor brains.

I sobbed listening to those words the millionth time.

Why is she so sensitive?

A cry baby!
Never knows how to take a joke.

That must have been so confusing for a little girl.

Divi Maggo

Why do you always cry on your birthday?

Too much to expect for my mother
to love me *one day* out of 365 days.

Too much to ask to not shout,
to not judge, to be gentle and warm.

Instead she threw parties that I never asked for,
got overstimulated and blamed me for making her work.

It was too much to ask
for calm and peace one day of the year.

Ugh! Birthdays are the hardest for me. How do you feel on your birthday? Do you associate a childhood experience/ feeling that makes you feel that way?

Divi Maggo

Let it go! They are your parents.

I have let it go. I have forgiven them.
But I will never forget the hurt.

I will not be their doormat.
Keeping the peace, making them happy.

I am expected to forgive
when there was never an apology.

But they are not expected to understand.
Just because they gave me life.

Wilted Flowers

As a woman I sympathize with my mother.

It must be suffocating
being in a loveless marriage,
working a sad job,
toxic people sucking your energy
day in and day out.

No joy, just responsibilities.

As a woman I admire your strength,
your courage to keep going,

But as a daughter, I am angry.
Angry that you let your sadness seep in me.

Angry that you poured that toxicity in me.
Your words still haunt me.

Like poison they lingered in my heart.
Your unkind voice became my inner voice.

I respect you for giving me everything.

But also heartbroken,
for all the things you took away.

Divi Maggo

I never cried with my mother.

But I did cry with my husband,
my friends, even my kids *over* my mother.

She thinks I have changed
since I created my own family.

I did, I did change.

Truth is, I finally found people
that stood by me while I stood up for myself.

My found family saved me.

Time for some gratitude! Let's take a pause and give a mini shout out to our found families. People that supported us when our families did not.

Divi Maggo

Why did you let your mother treat you like that?

Because I saw her scars too.
The ones she tried to hide behind anger and despair.

Her wounds pained me.
So I put her needs before mine.

Her happiness became my entire life's worth.

I am to blame too.
Stifled my voice for her smile.

Decades of healing,
I still feel guilty standing up for myself.

Wilted Flowers

My relationship with my mother
is like an ex-lover's.

Broken up ages ago.
But there are still tears when I talk about her.

Right person, wrong time.
Hoping we could have been together
if she just worked on herself.

I still miss the sound of her laughter.
Her smell and warm hugs.

I just wish the bad was not that bad.
Maybe in the next life.

Divi Maggo

I know I will cry the hardest when my mom dies.

But there will also be a sense of relief.
Relief that things will not get worse
from that day onwards.

Relief that maybe she will get
a better suited daughter in her next life.

Relief that we will not break
each other's hearts anymore.

Relief that at least one of us is finally at peace.

Wilted Flowers

I cannot even have a normal conversation
with my mother.

The everyday, the mundane
gets twisted and turned to fulfill her own version.

I envy the daughters
who are best friends with their mothers,
I have to think and rethink
what I should share with her.

Because everything ends in scrutiny,
making me feel less and unlovable.

It's torture.

Divi Maggo

My childhood wounds reopened in motherhood,
spilled out like guts from a carcass.

Before being a mother,
I rarely thought about my childhood.
I knew it wasn't perfect,
and that was that.

But when I saw my kids' beautiful faces,
innocent eyes and pure souls staring back,
I realized.

I realized how much cruelty
I had endured at the hands of my parents.

So I let out the little girl I had locked up long back.

I wiped her tears and hugged her.
I let her pour all that she ever wanted to say
but never could.

My kids saved the little and the adult me.

Why do you still hold onto things?
It has been decades?

Because the little girl is still sobbing from all the pain
and hurt you caused.

And I don't know how to make her *stop*.

Divi Maggo

Why is your family's honor in my vagina?

Why is that the person who sexually assaulted me is free
but I am in a prison - to never talk about what happened?

Your society's fake prison of rules and honor
can not drown my voice anymore.

This time I choose me.

And I will keep choosing me until my last breath.

Trigger warning: Did you experience sexual assault as a kid or a grown up? Did you tell anyone?
Write it down, it will make you feel better.

_____

_____

_____

_____

In my experience, sharing the trauma and talking to a therapist helped me get some of my power back. What do you think will help you get your power back?

_____

_____

_____

_____

_____

_____

_____

_____

Wilted Flowers

It is tiring being a woman.

Be a mom, be a boss.
Still a failure, never enough.

Always thinking how to not get stalked.
Not get raped.
Not get killed.

Suck your stomach in.
Pluck your eyebrows.
Straighten your curls.
Look like a *little girl* even when you are grown.

Be polite.
Cross your legs.
Know your place.

Smile like you mean it.
Cum like you mean it.
Even if you have to fake.

Boost his ego.
Stroke his muscles.
Rules, honor, society,
When is it enough?

It's tiring being a woman.
I am so very tired.

Divi Maggo

The oldest daughter.
"We never had to worry about her" daughter.

The one that
took her father's anger,
The one who
wiped her mother's tears.

The therapist.
The caregiver.
The afterthought.

The one who lived for others,
But called *selfish* for doing one thing for herself.

The oldest daughter,
The tired one.
The broken one.
The misused one.

Wilted Flowers

Why is it so difficult to find adult female friendships?

Friends that are the perfect combination of
ambition and womanhood.

Friends that want to grow,
and want you to grow with them.

Not shit at your dreams,
or flaky or jealous or judgemental.

Why is it so difficult to find good adult female
friendships?

I wish to go back to a life without calories.

I wish to go back to a life when I do not compare my reflection in every passing mirror.

I wish to go back to a life when I do not reflect on how *thin* I was in all the past photographs.

I wish I do not have to rethink everytime I eat.

I wish...

The *hate hate* relationship with fitting rooms,
I wonder when did it start?

When did the excitement of buying new clothes turn into
dread and anxiety, mostly ending in tears.

Why did we all grow up so broken?

Divi Maggo

Your mind is playing tricks at you again.
You do not look bigger just because you had *fun* on
vacation.

Food is more than weight.
It's full of experiences, memories, family recipes and
first time baking with kids.

You do not need to move more because you were *bad*
when you were making memories with your family.

Your body deserves more love.

What is the most hurtful thing you heard growing up that carved the way you see your physical body?

_____

_____

_____

_____

_____

_____

_____

_____

_____

_____

_____

_____

Divi Maggo

This is love, she screamed.

Her father winced, her mother mourned.
Her broken jaw and sore eyes were souvenirs of passion,
she said.

Her brother disapproved,
her sister cried.

She left the house, disheartened but willful.
They were not ready to see the fire within, she thought.

A few days later, a telegram was received.

Her bruised body had given out but the courageous heart
still loved.

*If you or anyone you know is suffering from domestic
violence, call 1.800.799.SAFE (7233)*

Wilted Flowers

Do you know what happens to good girls?
They die.

They might not be physically dead,
but they are mentally broken.

Their hearts and spirits are broken,
trying to please everyone.
Parents, teachers, friends, boyfriends.

When does it stop?
Is it worth it?
*Is it worth putting my hopes, dreams and happiness on
hold for yours?*

Teach your daughters,
she is an ocean.

She can raise a storm and drown thousands.

Teach your daughters,
she is mother earth.

She can love, nurture and provide life.

Teach your daughter to never fear to show both sides to
the world.

Wilted Flowers

From far, I was a *golden child*.

Perfect grades, perfect manners,
trophy for my parents.

Inside, I was slowly dying.
My anxiety was gnawing at my insides at all times.

Being good was the only source of my parents'
happiness.

So I had to strangle my dreams for theirs.

No friends, no heartbreaks;
Nothing that will distract you from perfection.

Did they even see me as human?
With human emotions and feelings?

Or was I just an epitome of control and obedience?

A trophy for their dreams.

What burdens did you feel from your parents growing up - academic, financial, emotional?

_____

_____

_____

_____

_____

Do you still make decisions from these burdens?
How do you separate yourself from them as an adult?

_____

_____

_____

_____

_____

_____

_____

Wilted Flowers

I wanted to be free of my thoughts,
but I slowly realized - I will never be free of them.

At least not in this lifetime.

So I poured them on paper,
and waited.

Slowly I found my people,
who were burnt same as me,
and in the process I found myself again.

Thank you for trusting me with your feelings,
thank you for honoring my words with your tears,
as you are healing you are healing me
and making my inner child smile.

Thank you!

Before we end the "feel" section, I have one last journal prompt for you.

Divi Maggo

If you could write a letter to your mom and tell her anything, what would you write? Don't hold back, be honest and let it out!

_____

_____

_____

_____

_____

_____

_____

_____

_____

_____

_____

_____

Wilted Flowers

Divi Maggo

Wilted Flowers

Divi Maggo

Heal

**So that your kids
do not have to heal from you...**

**Here is a Spotify playlist
to feel the love for your kids,
how special motherhood can be,
how fast time is going.**

Divi Maggo

Motherhood cracked open my heart,
in the best way possible.

My kids healed parts of me
that I didn't even know were broken.

I opened my eyes
and saw the world for the very first time.

The unconditional love you feel in your bones,
in your skin, in your veins pumping your blood.

Their innocence, their soft love
will make you fight Gods.

It will make you want to change the world,
make it a better place for them.

Their soft glances, when they just melt in your arms,
their small feet and clear sparkle in the eyes,
it will make your heart skip a beat.

I wonder how are we worthy to take care of something
so pure and full of love.

Every breath I take will be in debt to them.

Wilted Flowers

To the mama nap trapped with her baby.

Isn't it beautiful when you can feel their warmth on you?

Isn't it beautiful when they fight sleep just to look at you
one more time?

Isn't it magical that you are their safe space,
where their bodies feel secure and minds feel at ease?

Your heartbeats in sync one more time.

Motherhood is pure magic.

Divi Maggo

Mommy, can you cover me up?
My son asks me every night.

My tired body sighs but my heart glows with warmth.

I tuck him in every night and give him a kiss good night.
He sleeps with a smile on his face.

I know he will grow out of it one day.

And ten years down the lane,
when I ask him,
can I tuck you in today?

I hope he says yes,
and give this old mother's withered heart
a warm glow again.

Wilted Flowers

Wait till you have kids
that behave just like you.

But I did.
I did have kids that are just like me.

And I realized
how easy it was to love me.

How easy it was to be kind,
to not belittle and humiliate.

I have kids that are just like me,
but they will never feel my heartbreak.

Think and write all the ways your kids are similar to you - how they act, how they feel.

_____

_____

_____

_____

_____

_____

_____

For what behaviors as a child you were shamed, screamed at, spanked, hit or isolated?

_____

_____

_____

_____

_____

_____

_____

_____

_____

What steps are you taking everyday to nourish that part of your kids - not repeating the patterns?

_____

_____

_____

_____

_____

_____

Divi Maggo

How you treat your child when they are small,
is how they will treat you once they grow up.

How you treat your child
when they asked you to play with you,
is how they will respond
when you ask them for dinner later.

How you treat your child when they had no one,
is how they will treat you when you have no one.

Wilted Flowers

My sweet child,
I will fight Gods and Monsters for you.

You will never have to beg for my love.

I will never drown you in my sorrows
or stifle your voice.

I will be the wind beneath your wings,
your freedom in the breezes of sky.

Divi Maggo

Teach your sons to be soft.
The world is full of macho men.

Teach them to be gentle,
teach them to be sweet.

Teach them the value of flowers,
the magic of forehead kisses.

Teach them about love,
teach them about smiles.

Teach them about books and coffee dates,
teach them about nature,
the trees, the ocean, the lakes.

And the world will heal.

Teach your daughters to love deeply.

Teach your sons to love gently.

Teach everyone
to not be a footnote in someone else's story.

Divi Maggo

I made the decision to bring you into this world.

I owe everything to you,
you don't owe me anything.

You don't have to earn my love.

You are not too *sensitive*,
too *wild* or *too much to handle*.
You are perfect the way you are.

You are my unicorn, rainbow
and butterflies combined.

I am grateful for you with every breath.

Do our kids owe us anything for bringing them into this world? How would you visualize your and your kids' relationship when they are adults?

What active steps are you taking to bring that relationship goal to fruition?

_____

_____

_____

_____

_____

_____

_____

_____

_____

_____

_____

_____

_____

Wilted Flowers

It's too hard to choose the best memory
I have of my dad growing up.

Tucking my feet under the blanket
while I sleep every night?

Gently waking me every morning
with warm water and warm milk in bed?

Buying magazines to do my hair
even when I was in high school?

Cooking my favorite food?

Never shouting, humiliating.

Why couldn't my mom be like that?

Divi Maggo

Your kids will remember all the kind things you did.

Unfortunately, they will also remember
each and every unkind thing you did.

But they will give you a million chances
to replace your unkind things with kind things.

It is up to you if you take it.

Wilted Flowers

Your kids do not need fancy clothes,
expensive toys or hundreds of vacations.

They do not care about brands
or if they have been to the Caribbean.

What they do need is your love,
say it to them, show it to them.

Show them you are kind,
show them you are accepting,
encourage their dreams.

Make their home a place of
warmth, peace and hope.

Divi Maggo

Make childhood memories
instead of childhood trauma.

Your kids are your Nobel prizes, Oscars combined.

Thirty years down the road,
when your kids miss you,
when they ask you to be in their kids lives,
that will be your success.

They should be homesick when they move away,
not *wanting* to get away.

You bring them in this world,
you owe them love.

Wilted Flowers

Wrote this poem for a mother suffering with cancer who
wanted to repair her relationship with her daughter before she
passed but did not know how/where to start.

I am sorry I was not the best mother.
I am sorry it took me so long to realize I made mistakes.

I am on borrowed time,
but if there is a God in this universe,
I will beg on my knees until my dying breath,
to shower you with love.

To touch your beautiful face and ask for forgiveness.
To hug you and give you a million kisses.

My intentions were good, my heart was pure.

I might have not broken all the generational curses
but I did break some.

Even if you don't see me,
I will be watching over you.

Every beautiful sunset, every rainbow,
every colorful butterfly
would be me telling you one last time,
I love you.

Divi Maggo

If you get to know you have 24 hours left on this Earth, how will you spend them? What will you say to your kids?

_____

_____

_____

_____

_____

_____

_____

_____

_____

_____

_____

_____

Now go and say it to them (your kids and loved ones).
We are all on borrowed time and tomorrow is not
promised.
Come back and write how they responded.

Divi Maggo

Your kids will break your heart one day,
then you will realize.

Even *if* my kids break my heart
everyday for the rest of my life,
I will still love them.

I will still be kind.

I will hug them and kiss them
and ask them what did I do wrong?

If they break my heart, so what?
They already gave me magic, love, healing.

They do not owe me anything.

Your motherhood will outlive you.

It's up to you if your parenting instills confidence in your child or anxiety and insecurities.

Your parenting will decide if your kids want to keep you in their lives and your grandkids lives in future.

Your motherhood will become your kids' inner voice.

It's up to you if that voice is kind and loving.

Divi Maggo

Your kids are not here to fulfill your dreams.

They are not here to achieve
what you could not achieve.

Your responsibilities and burdens
should not be on their tiny shoulders.

Your kids are not here to heal your trauma,
to carry your emotional and financial baggage.

Your kids are their own person.

Stop viewing them as your extension.

Wilted Flowers

My parents thought I was a non affectionate child.

Little did they know,
I used to cry alone in my room for their affection.

My mother never hugged me,
never said I love you.

People say I *baby* my kids too much.
I kiss them too much,
I hug them too much.

I would rather be *a too much parent*,
than my kids crying alone for my affection.

**Do you know your kids' love language? What actions
do you take to nurture them and show them
affection/love?**

_____

_____

_____

_____

_____

_____

_____

_____

_____

_____

_____

_____

Wilted Flowers

Check on your *good kids*,
the *"we never have to worry about"* kids.

Your *golden child*,
the old soul,
mature for their age kids.

We are not doing good,
the pressure and expectations are getting to us.

Exchanged our childhood
for our parent's happiness.

Now we are people pleasers
with crippling anxiety and unintentional tears.

Check on your good kids,
tell them it's okay to make mistakes.

Tell them you will love them regardless.
Hug them tight and ask them to breathe.

They need you more than they show.

Divi Maggo

And suddenly you turned 5.

Yesterday we were fussing about you not latching,
pacifiers, burp clothes, diapers, bottles, formula.

Today we saw you walk at your Pre-K graduation.
Head held high, hugging your teachers
and laughing with friends.

How did these last five years go by so fast?
I am scared, I want time to freeze.

But it keeps slipping away.
Leaving me with memories etched in my brain.

It's getting more difficult to lift you,
but I still do.
The body wants to give in but the mother's heart keeps
holding on.

I grieve the baby, the toddler
but proud of the kid in front of me.

The kind, hearty, soft, loving boy.
I wish this world gives you peace.

Wilted Flowers

We are parents, we can never be wrong.

I wonder how many parents lose their kids because they
could never be *wrong*.

I wonder how many kids cry themselves to sleep every
night because their parents always need to be right.

How many dreams shatter everyday,
innocence lost, forever scars on their little bodies and
fragile hearts.

Because love lost the battle to obedience, control and
being right.

Divi Maggo

My parents said they always provided a safe space to
communicate.

They did not.

Most days the only conversation they had with me was if
I finished my chores,
and what grades I got.

Never about how I am feeling,
am I sad or happy or angry or anxious?

Feelings are for pussies, crying is for the weak.

Meanwhile in my room,
I am screaming, crying in the pillow.
to not make a noise,
to not be a burden.

Whole body shaking with anxiety of living
in the *safe space* they provided.

That house never felt like home.

Wilted Flowers

Mommy, I will be all alone when I grow up.
My son said while playing with his cars.

It took me by surprise.
Guilt ridden,
I sat near him and asked him what he meant by that.

That's how life is, you grow up and move away from your parents.

Tearing up, I hugged him.
Being an immigrant with no family around is hard but
it's harder for the kids.

I promise little one I will follow you around the world
and never let you feel alone.

A promise from a wounded mother.

**Have you talked to your kids about your relationship
with your parents? How honest were you and how did
your kids respond?**

Wilted Flowers

Your kids will figure you out one day.

They will see you as a human,
with flaws and trauma.

Grief that oozed out of you into their lives.

Every tiny tear you tried to hide,
every rip in your heart,
every ache in your soul.

So heal for them.
Heal because they deserve your best version.

Heal so that they don't have to heal *from you*.

Divi Maggo

How would you feel if your kids blame you for their
traumas in future?

I will be hurt but not for the reason you think.

I will be hurt that I failed to give them a safe
environment to talk about my shortcomings.

I will be angry that I missed all the signs of their
unhappiness.

I will hug them and ask for their forgiveness.

And I will be at their doorstep everyday,
with coffee and sweets to talk it through.

I would not blame them,
I would not be angry,
I would not play the victim and isolate them for being
bad kids.

I love them more than my ego,
and when I say I love them unconditionally,
I mean it.

Wilted Flowers

Growing up, I was an addict.

My drug of choice was pleasing my mother.

I was her puppet and she was my master.

I would do everything to please her,
to make her happy.
But it was never enough.

She would resort to being sad,
screaming day in and day out.

We have to keep mommy happy.
My father used to say.
Slap a smile and do as she says.

Decades later, she is still sad.
And I am all grown up,
a broken shell with a grieving inner child.

An addict trying to quit pleasing her mother.

Divi Maggo

My mom wanted me
to be a "big person" when I grow up.

While she was spinning big dreams for me,
dreams that will solve all "her" problems.

I was dreaming of a home,
with no screaming and humiliation.

Where no one cries
themselves to sleep every night.

Where there is no trauma.
A place of love and warmth.
A home not a prison of "dreams".

Wilted Flowers

Your mother did not heal her childhood wounds.
She repeated the cycle
and inflicted the same pain she endured.

She chose her comfort of toxicity,
her ego, her self righteousness.

Kept the "blood" family close
even if they hurt her daughter.

The saddest part is,
she would do it all over again
in the name of *we did our best.*

Divi Maggo

Suck it up, trauma makes you stronger.

Did it make me stronger?
I wonder, lying in bed crying over lost childhood in my
thirties.

Did it make the little girl stronger?
That lost her innocence at the age of nine
and cried herself to sleep every night.

No, trauma did not make her stronger.
But it did make her feel worthless, guilty and shameful.

Wilted Flowers

Wait until your kids break your heart one day,
then you will remember me!

They might break my heart.
I will still be in their forever debt,
giving a lost soul like me unconditional pure love.

They taped back the broken shell of a person,
piece by piece,
and day by day I healed.

And I only hope even if they break my heart one day,
our love will help me tape it back again.

Divi Maggo

Prior gifted kids, how are you doing?

Are you burnt out yet?
Or are you still riding the *overburdened* wave?

Every big milestone is just another checkmark,
no celebration, just a sigh of relief.

Does resting give you anxiety?

Did you also miss out on experiences
because of your *perfectionism*?

I hope we find peace one day.

When I am at peace,
my kids are at peace.

When I am happy,
my kids are happy.

Their happiness and peace
depends on my happiness and peace,
maybe just for a few years.

And I will fight everything and everyone on God's green
earth to protect their peace and happiness.

Divi Maggo

This Mother's Day,
keep the mothers in prayers that lost their babies to wars.

Hold your babies tight for the mothers that will never be
able to hold their babies again.

Give your babies extra kisses for the mothers that could
not even kiss their babies goodbye.

Read your babies one more bedtime story for the mother
who could not even tuck their kids lifeless bodies.

This Mother's Day,
weep for the mothers who can't weep anymore.

The tears have dried.
The soul is lost.

Wilted Flowers

How do I sing happy birthday to my kids when there are
beheaded babies in this world?

How do I explain to my kids why I cry when looking at
my phone these days?

How do I keep this rage and sadness in me managed to
keep being a civilized member of the society?

Is this what you call "justice"?
Beheaded babies and pregnant women burnt alive?

For the wars, genocides, infanticides, crimes against
children happening in the world,
I shed tears with you every night.

Write a letter to your kids, something they can read in future. What are your hopes and dreams for their lives?

_____

_____

_____

_____

_____

_____

_____

_____

_____

_____

_____

The future is bright

Why you ask?
because you have forgotten
you are a bad bitch,
overcoming generational traumas
one day at a time...

You deserve love,
you deserve everything you ever dreamt of.

I created a Spotify playlist that will make you feel
powerful, a baddie and trust the universe:

Divi Maggo

Dear husband,

I would do this life with you,
all over again.

The sleepless nights,
the diapers,
the crying,
the meltdowns.

Drowning in work,
hustling in careers,
running on coffee, fumes,
hugs and kisses.

I will choose you, love you, kiss you and hold you,
all over again.

Until I meet you again in the next life,
and do all of this all over again.

Wilted Flowers

Do you know how beautiful it is?

To love every waking minute of this life,
melting in your arms.

To breathe the same air as you.

To dream with you, to create a life with you.

You had my heart a long time ago,
but now you have my soul.

Divi Maggo

Praying to God with every heartbeat.

Give him all my happiness,
give me all his pain and sufferings.

Give him my breath, my health, my life, my heaven.

Give me his sickness, his death, his hell.

Give him my love,
give him my lust,
give him my soul.

This is a love of many lifetimes.

Wilted Flowers

And in the end,
I would have bled myself dry.
Just to save you from yourself.

This one is for my cousin who took her own life.
She was a victim of domestic violence.
She did tell some of our family members what she was
going through.
She was asked to adjust and it will get better with time.
It did not get better and she had to take a drastic step to
get out of this situation.

I miss her everyday.
I will keep using my voice to speak out.

If you or anyone you know is suffering from domestic
violence, call 1.800.799.SAFE (7233)

If you or anyone you know are having bad thoughts,
call 988 Suicide & Crisis Lifeline

Divi Maggo

When all your life you have received conditional love
from your parents, society, friends.

And someone comes along who loves you for you.

Not because you are perfect,
not because of your achievements,
not because of your obedience.

You finally feel at peace.

Wilted Flowers

When they are screaming at your face,
Pause.

Pause and look them up and down.
Imagine your guardian angels
standing beside you, protecting you.

Think of all their insecurities
that they are projecting on you.

Control your emotions.
Stand tall.
Give a sly smile like you pity them.

And move on.

The best reaction is no reaction.

Divi Maggo

Peace was never her forte.

She was born to ignite old flames
and stir new revolutions.

Wilted Flowers

All are lost,
but only some are scared.

Are you ready to lose *yourself* to find *yourself*?

Divi Maggo

I will be remembered as the woman
who never kept her mouth shut.

And I am okay with that.

Dream big.
Dream outrageous.

If your dreams are not making people uncomfortable,
you are not dreaming big enough.

Your dreams are for you.
Only you can fuel your dreams.

Surround yourself with people who have achieved what
you want to achieve.

Talk big and do even bigger.
Surprise yourself.
Break glass ceilings.
The world is your oyster.

Divi Maggo

Your bad memories will always be with you.

They will hit you like a freight train,
when you think you are doing good.

What you do when the trauma hits you is what matters.

Do you let it spiral out of control?

Do you push it down and dissociate
with people or things?

Or do you sit with it?

Let it wash over you,
but instead of drowning, you float.

Man vs Bear.
Man vs Bear.
Man vs Bear.

Don't underestimate my unhealed trauma
and unfiltered rage.

There are days when my lack of fear of dying can take
both Man and Bear.

Divi Maggo

If you are trying to improve your life,
be dangerous.

Flirt with destiny,
marry the risk.

Not being comfortable
is your friend.

Surprise yourself,
then surprise some more.

You were meant to do hard things.
You were meant to be invincible.

The black sheep,
the one that people do not understand.

Your future is calling.

It is not wrong to want success for your art.

It is not wrong to want big money for your art.

It is not wrong to want something more than a 9-5.

Desiring money, fame, success doesn't make you less of a storyteller, creator, artist.

Why are you chained to the ground?
When you can soar like a bird.

Divi Maggo

Whatever is yours,
will come back to you.

Whatever is not,
will never stay.

Read it again.

P.S - your future self.

Think back to the things you did not get -
love, job, degree.

Did *you* want them or were you mirroring other's
expectations? Society, parents, spouse, kids.

Now, you *not* getting the thing,
Did it end up being better?

Divi Maggo

Somewhere along the way,
I stopped loving myself.

And I started trying to perfect myself.

Don't eat too much chocolate,
don't drink too much,
don't sleep too late,
don't scroll too much.

The *clean girl* aesthetic,
the *trad wife* aesthetic.

What happened to just having fun?

What happened to living in the moment?

Wilted Flowers

Please stay.

I know it's hard,
I know it's messy,
I know the hurt, the pain.

Still stay.

You will love again,
you will laugh again.

The pain will heal,
time will be your friend.

Please stay.
your friends need you,
your family needs you,
please, please stay.

Divi Maggo

Healing will be lonely.

You will lose friends, family, jobs,
dreams you realized were never yours.

But you will receive so much back.

Love from your inner child,
spark in your eyes,
color and hope for the future.

It will be a rebirth.
A new version of you.
calm, dreamy and free.

You meet your future self for a coffee date.

What do they say?

What are they wearing?

Are they sad?
Are they happy?
Are they fulfilled?

Divi Maggo

I am so distracted at my 9-5
that it scares me sometimes.

Like the kid sitting in a classroom
looking outside the window,
at the birds flying by - free.

I yearn to be free.
Free in nature, free in time,
free to be with loved ones.

Because the future is not promised.
And I will not die with regrets.

Wilted Flowers

You can feel it in your bones, in your veins.
In the blood pumping through your body.

You can feel your dreams turning into reality.

You can smell the victories,
the endless possibilities.

You are not surviving,
you are thriving.

Divi Maggo

For my fellow Booktok girlies:

Beware of me, I am a reader.

I breathe fictional worlds and love characters more than
real people.

I feel too much and love too deeply.

I mourn characters' death and fight alongside them,
in kingdoms far far away.

I will ghost you for a good book,
and a nice cup of coffee.

Beware of me, I am a reader.

What are your far fetched dreams? You know dreams that even your subconscious laughs at you for having them. Don't hold back!

_____

_____

_____

_____

_____

_____

_____

_____

_____

_____

_____

Divi Maggo

Not a knight in shining armor,
not a white horse savior.

A soldier of darkness.

The princess saved herself in this one.

Wilted Flowers

We are like the sun and the moon.

One shines bright, king of all things illuminating.

The other is the triumphant queen of darkness.

Still caressing each other
in moments of dawn and dusk.

Divi Maggo

Heart full of gold,
head full of dreams.

A lost wanderer, they called her.

A cosmic miracle intoxicated with
Love, Hope and Magic.

Wilted Flowers

There are days
when I breathe in sunshine.

Then there are days
when darkness welcomes an old friend home.

Divi Maggo

Pain is a beautiful thing,
it bursts open hearts,
letting the words flow out from the cracks.

For only the moon knew her darkest secrets.
And the stars danced in her fantasies.

Dear heart,

Dance in the glory of madness.

Bask in the shadows of chaos.

Dive in the mysteries of kismet.

Celebrate the magic within.

Wilted Flowers

A new soul will rise
from your burning aspirations,
like a phoenix rising from its own ashes.

Divi Maggo

Sunshine and rainbows were not her forte.
She longed for lightning and thunderstorms.

Courageous, bold, passionate, inspiring.

She yearned for something
to electrify her soul.

Wilted Flowers

She had the soul of a butterfly.
Breathtakingly beautiful
but one could not hold her.

For she will fly away to distant lands,
searching for sweet bliss.

And in death,
her beauty will adorn the pages of
poems and love letters.

Divi Maggo

And sometimes I feel my future self was with me,
when I used to cry myself to sleep every night.

How else would you explain me being alive today?

Even when the heart
was shattered in a million pieces,

I trusted my future self to glue it all back together.

My inner child trusted my future self then.
Just as I trust my future self now.

Wilted Flowers

Divi Maggo

Thank you!

You have reached the end of my first book. I cannot thank you enough for giving me a platform to help people maneuver these heavy and difficult feelings.

Growing up, I always felt alone and misunderstood. I remember in middle school I tried to share how hurt I am with things at home. I was made fun of and shamed that made me feel even smaller.

It was not until I became a mother that all of these feelings, hurt came to the surface again and I knew I had to work through them to not repeat the pattern.

I started therapy, journaling, creating healthy boundaries and of course writing. This book here is a physical manifestation of my healing in progress.

When I started writing, I thought I would be shunned and made fun of but something beautiful happened. I found a community of people hurting the same way I am hurting. It gave me hope and it gave me strength to keep going.

These wounds are heavy and deep. It would take a village to learn how to live with them.

Thank you for being my village.

Divi Maggo

"Wilted flowers" is a collection of poems about navigating motherhood with a mother-wound.

Why the name "Wilted Flowers"?
Because even though we are a bit wilted by our childhood traumas. We can be full and green again if we water ourselves enough.

This book belongs to you if you have emotional and psychological pain from difficult and strained relationships with your mother or motherly figure.

This book belongs to you if you feel ashamed and guilty for being low contact or no contact with your mother.

This book belongs to you if you have childhood trauma and were hurt (verbally, emotionally, mentally or physically) by your parents growing up.

Follow the writer on social media
to stay connected on future projects:

Instagram: divi_maggo
Tiktok: divi_maggo
Facebook: divi_maggo

Made in the USA
Las Vegas, NV
17 August 2024

93977438R10095